Cultivating System Change

A Practitioner's Companion

Anna Birney

Head of System Innovation Lab
Forum for the Future
www.forumforthefuture.org

 **Routledge**
Taylor & Francis Group

LONDON AND NEW YORK

First published 2014 by Greenleaf Publishing Limited

Published 2017 by Routledge
2 Park Square, Milton Park, Abingdon, Oxon OX14 4RN
605 Third Avenue, New York, NY 10017

*Routledge is an imprint of the Taylor & Francis Group,
an informa business*

ISBN 13: 978-1-910174-09-8 (pbk)

A catalogue record for this title is available from the British Library.

Page design and typesetting by Alison Rayner
Cover by Becky Chilcott

Abstract

THIS BOOK PROVIDES AN INTRODUCTION to the world of systems change. There exists a large and diverse number of practitioners across various sectors who are exploring what systems change means for them. This book de-mystifies dense, hard-to-read, research on systems thinking and sustainability transitions so as to support an individual, group or organisation's venture into this work.

It gives an overview of the frameworks and models that exist and offers strategies and examples of how to set about creating change. It is there to support you with key questions and tips to guide your way. If you have reached the limits of what you or your organisation can do and want to be at the leading edge of sustainability then this book is for you.

About the Author

ANNA BIRNEY is Head of Forum for the Future's (**www.forumforthefuture.org**) System Innovation Lab. Forum works globally with business, government and others to solve complex challenges so as to transform essential systems like food and energy to secure a sustainable future. The Lab (**www.forumforthefuture.org/the-lab**) is where we experiment and learn how we and others create system change. Anna is passionate about developing and facilitating programmes for individuals, organisations and systems to discover innovative approaches to change.

Anna began seeking system change when working on multi-stakeholder processes around the UN World Summit on Sustainable Development and across the education system (**www.forumforthefuture.org/blog/ challenge-accelerating-change-across-systems**) at WWF-UK. Since joining Forum in 2008 she has worked on business and sector strategies, motivating leaders and experimenting with approaches to scaling up change. This includes working with the Shell Foundation (**www.forumforthefuture. org/project/scaling-success/more/ethical-agents**) to maximise the reach and impact of 'ethical agents' in retail markets, working to shape the health system with the NHS and Bupa, and being a design and learning partner on other sector based projects including the Sustainable Shipping Initiative (**www.ssi2040.org**), Futurescapes (**www.forumforthefuture.org/ project/futurescapes/overview**), Community Energy Coalition (**www.forum**

forthefuture.org/project/community-energy-coalition/overview) and The Smart CSOs Lab (**www.smart-csos.org**).

Anna provides advice and direction on Golden's global Ecosystems Labs. She has a Postgraduate Diploma in action research from the University of Bath's Management School and is completing a doctorate on 'How might people and organizations, who seek a sustainable future, cultivate systemic change?' from Lancaster University Management School.

....

Acknowledgments

FIRST AND FOREMOST I would like to thank my husband for the practical and emotional support he has given – and continues to give – me on my life's work. I would also like to thank all my wonderful colleagues, tutors, partners and friends who have helped me develop the ideas and actions found in this book. I wrote this book so I can turn to my children and say I tried.

Contents

CONTENTS

Preface

I CAN REMEMBER SITTING in the cavernous underground plenary hall of the UN in New York in 2002 watching multiple governments negotiate text for the World Summit for Sustainable Development and thinking how can one person like me possibly start to effect change across the global education system?

My experience led me to the conclusion that spending my hours watching and trying to influence what was said in UN text was not the way to do it. So where does one even start?

I am fascinated by why people are inspired to make the world a better place and what will enable more people to make this an explicit part of their work. It often starts with hugely ambitious goals or complex, tangled-up problems, but in both cases they can leave us paralysed into non-action or, worse still, repeating the same mistakes over and over again.

A formative part of my journey has been weaving in and out of the education system working with my colleagues as we attempted many strategies, from supporting individual schools, training leaders, creating frameworks and communicating success to trying to influence governments and the UN.

We did have some success including influencing the UK government's sustainable schools agenda and the UN decade for education for sustainable development. As new national governments drive things in different directions what I am inspired by is the multitude of amazing leaders I have been privileged to work with who really want to see a deeper shift within the education system. They are trying to transform the education of their pupils by providing them with the skills to deal with an uncertain future and developing organisational strategies and forms of learning that demonstrate a new model of education.

My insight through this work is the importance of being a cultivator of system change. When working to create spaces to experiment and learn, and setting up communities of practice with school leaders, the metaphor of cultivating a garden has proved a useful one. In a garden you cannot predict or control all that happens; there are some factors you have to live and work with, such as sunlight, rain, the rhythm of the seasons. You can, however, still grow, guide, water, prune and have some influence over what happens.

This book is a culmination of the practice in education and the work I have done across different systems such as health, food, energy and mobility and with different types of organisations including business, the public sector, foundations and not-for-profits. It also reflects the inquiry I have been following through my PhD. As I move to finish that thesis this book is one way to support better actions, strategies and outcomes in order that academia fulfils its promise of improving practical knowledge rather than producing yet more elite and hard-to-access research.

....

Introduction

AS MORE AND MORE PEOPLE and organisations are asking the question 'where do I start if I want to work on these massive systemic challenges or shift global systems?' this book offers an introduction to system change theory and strategies and provides practical examples of what organisations are starting to do. It offers some reflections and suggestions about how you might start to navigate and create your own way to cultivate system change.

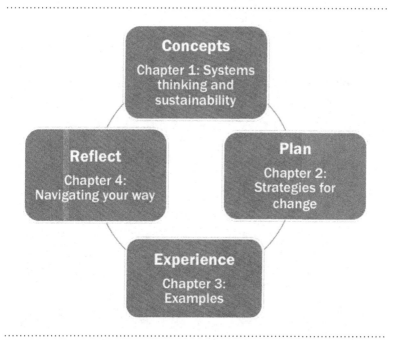

Concepts — Chapter 1: Systems thinking and sustainability

Reflect — Chapter 4: Navigating your way

Plan — Chapter 2: Strategies for change

Experience — Chapter 3: Examples

The book consists of four sections. Chapter 1 provides the bigger picture of systems thinking, especially how we can use a 'living systems' perspective as a tool to understanding sustainability and how we might create change. Chapter 2 pulls strategies for action from a multitude of theoretical models. Chapter 3 illustrates how organisations are implementing these strategies. Chapter 4 provides tips for you as a practitioner navigating this territory.

Finally, questioning is a driving force behind learning. Many of the ideas behind cultivating system change can be difficult to understand until you practise them. Therefore, I have included questions to prompt reflections and move to action. In this way I hope this book serves as a practical companion.

I look forward to the continued conversation and to hear what people are doing and learning.

Twitter: @AnnasQuestions #systemchange

CHAPTER 1

Taking a Living Systems Perspective

WE NEED A NEW APPROACH to addressing the challenges of sustainability, which can be characterised as the failure of humans and the social systems they create to recognise they are part of the larger ecological system. As we get closer to ecological tipping points the challenge is one of human choice.

This chapter shows why we need to choose a living systems perspective, which means:

- Seeking the whole system view which recognises ourselves and our society are nested within our environment;

- Taking a relationship-based approach to cultivating change; and

- Learning and innovating towards a sustainable future.

Systems thinking

We are living in a world of ever-growing complexity. The whole of humanity on Earth is becoming more noticeably interdependent. Global communications, international governance, markets and supply chains make us increasingly interconnected. We are also faced with mounting dilemmas of sustainability, as inequality grows and we push up against our environmental limits and thus risk destroying our life support systems.

This has never been as acutely demonstrated as through the effects of climate change where the challenge is truly global and affects us all, rich and poor. It can seem at times that we are locked into this trajectory. As a society we are putting more and more energy into repeating the same behaviours. We are struggling to find strategies and solutions to match the challenge.

Question: What strategies and approaches are you frustrated by that do not seem to address the urgency and scale of the challenge?

> *'The world is a complex, interconnected finite, ecological-social-psychological-economic system. We treat it as if it were not, as it were divisible, separable, simple and infinite. Our persistent, intractable, global problems arise directly from this mismatch.'*[1]

Systems thinking is one approach that might help us shift our perspective when trying to address the challenges of sustainability. *A system is '. . . a set of things – people, cells, molecules or whatever – interconnected in such a way that they produce their own pattern of behaviour over time'.*[2]

Systems thinking focuses our attention not on the parts of the system but on how the parts work and operate together through their interconnectivity and relationships.

The kind of systems thinking that I find most useful draws on complexity theory and living systems analysis.[3] This living systems perspective appreciates there is a deep structure of reality, or a pattern that connects all living creatures to the planet. The pattern that connects is that we are alive.

Living systems: Lessons from ecology

We can understand living systems through these three qualities[4] – nested whole systems, resilience and self-organisation.

Nested whole systems

Living systems are embedded or nested within each other. Take your body for example: your stomach and digestive system are systems nested within your body. Our social system is embedded in our ecology. The retail sector is nested within our economy, the food system within our society as a whole.

'Life started with single-cell bacteria, not with elephants.'[5]

This quality is what we 'see' when we look at a system. Most of the time when we 'see' a system it is dynamically stable. There are times however where new systems emerge. This evolution happens from the bottom up and when it does the emergent result is a new whole system. In nature you do not see systems that are partial – for example, a 'nearly eye' or 'almost heart'.

To ensure systems are functioning optimally we need to understand that the larger layers serve the purpose of the nested sub-systems. For example, our body serves to support its cells. If this malfunctions, such as when cells break free and multiply exponentially causing cancer, the wider system (or our body in this case) malfunctions.

Recognising the nested nature of systems and paying attention to their alignment enables them to flourish.

Question: Think of a challenge you are trying to address at the moment.

What happens when you step back and consider it within a wider system? Can you map the pattern?

Resilience and the importance of relationships

Although our systems seem stable, on closer inspection they are in constant flow. Using the example of our bodies again blood and nerve signals are constantly flowing. There are multiple feedback loops, relationships and interconnections that maintain its current state. When we cut our skin the blood causes a clot and works to restore and rebuild. Living systems may be stable but they are far from equilibrium.[6]

You characterise these relationships as a system's resilience.

How resilient a system is depends on the multiplicity, diversity and variability of the relationships. The more of these a system has, the more resilient it is to shocks and changes. There are limits to this resilience. When it reaches these limits a system will tip or shift from one dynamic state to another. This shift means existing connections move around and reconnect in new ways. It becomes a radically different system from what existed before, as when fish stocks disappear or after the fall of the Roman Empire.

Question: What examples of a system tipping can you think of? What are the stable systems you rely on and what would happen if they tipped?

Self-organisation and learning at the heart of human life

If systems are dynamic, up until the point when they shift or a new system emerges, what drives them?

There is no evidence that there is an evolutionary plan; and yet we continually regenerate and evolve. This process is called self-organisation. Self-organisation is guided by a simple principle – life's inherent tendency to create novelty.[7]

Humans create novelty through processes of innovation and learning. We are constantly trying out new ideas and actions, deliberately or not, some creating better results than others, so that we learn, adapt and evolve.

Question: Through history what innovations have driven wider change? What are some of the positive and negative impacts?

Sustainability: A systemic challenge

By exploring sustainability through the three qualities of a living system we can see why it is a living systems challenge and therefore why its perspective could be useful when seeking to cultivate a sustainable future.

Society nested in nature

> *'Man talks of a battle with nature, forgetting that if he won that battle he would find himself on the losing side'*
> ECONOMIST FRITZ SCHUMACHER

The challenge of sustainability is often characterised as the failure of humans and the social systems we create (such as the economy) to recognise they are sub-systems of the larger ecological system. As we pursue goals of growth in our socio-economic sub-systems, which requires a constant throughput of environmental resources, we are starting to overshoot the carrying capacity of the environment. This will ultimately mean our ecological support system will malfunction.

We need, therefore, to take a nested whole system perspective. Standard models of sustainability such as the three pillars of sustainability or the three overlapping circles of social, environment and economy are inadequate as they do not speak of the need to work within the ecological system and its limits. Instead, this can be represented in the nested diagram of the economy, nested within the social world, nested within the environment.

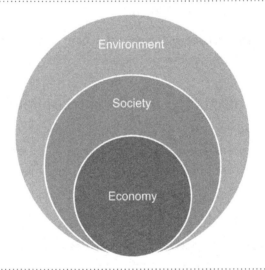

Question: What examples are there of socio-economic sub-systems not working within environmental limits?

Our reduced resilience can lead to tipping points

'The organisation that destroys its environment destroys itself'
EARLY SYSTEMS THEORIST GREGORY BATESON

Our world (and therefore our existence) is maintained by the multitude of relationships that keeps it dynamically stable and resilient to changes. We rely on our ecological life support system to maintain certain functions so that we can live and survive on this planet: clean water, fertile soil and a stable climate.

Many writers, commentators and scientists are stating this resilience is being eroded. In our atmospheric system, for example, we are moving closer and closer to the point where it will be disrupted in an irreversible fashion. We are getting closer to the tipping point.

'Non-linear systems are riddled with tipping points, but often a system is so complex that it is impossible to know exactly when these will be encountered.'[8]

We do not know when the thresholds of our ecological system might suddenly shift. For climate change it is suggested that 2 degrees Celsius might be the global limit of overall temperature rise beyond which we will witness irreversible change. Others say we have already reached that point in relation to carbon dioxide in the atmosphere. Wherever we stand on this, we still need to change our path, take a living systems perspective and increase our resilience.

Question: How close do you believe we are to a critical tipping point? Do you think we can change the path we are currently on?

Can we learn our way out?

'Climate change cannot be tackled by technical, economic and political measures alone... the real challenge of climate change. .. is it throws us down against ourselves. The bottom line and top priority is that we must get to grips with the roots of life.'[9]

The sustainability challenge is not an environmental one. The planet is perfectly capable of looking after itself. The question is whether humans will survive as a species on it and with what quality of life?

The future is not written. We can choose our path.

Question: What are your hopes and fears for the future? What future do you want?

What does it mean to take a living system perspective?

'Nothing is permanent but change'
HERACLITUS

The old view was adequate but the new one is more adequate

The way we see the world shapes how we understand and the actions we choose to take. The dominant perspective over the past couple of centuries has seen the world as no more than a resource to exploit. This perspective, manifested in our institutions and economy, has brought us to the brink and threatens our societies across the world.[10]

Our society is ever-changing. We have moved from a foraging, to an agrarian, to an industrial and now to an information society. Through the process of learning and innovation we have repeatedly reconstructed the world in the face of dilemmas.

In the face of sustainability challenges can we start to see ourselves as part of a living system and pay attention to how we cultivate relationships, learn and innovate towards a sustainable future?

CHAPTER 2

Developing Strategies for Change

IT IS ALL VERY WELL SAYING one must take a living systems perspective but how does that translate into strategies that help guide action? Many practitioners want to know where they can direct their effort. If we take the three qualities of a living systems perspective it means we need to look at models that look at nested or multi-layers within the systems. We also need to explore how they tip, the role different actors play, and how to support actors to build relationships that cultivate change.

Finally, we will need learning processes to support transformational practices and emerging leaders. In this chapter I have taken some of the key theories and models that different system change practitioners use.

Question: What models and strategies are you using for change? Why are they useful and what are their limitations?

I have found that there are commonalities between these theories which can be presented as six strategies to support a practitioner to cultivate system change.

The strategies

1. Identify the different **actors** in a system. Engage leaders and people who might build a new system from a diverse set of people.

Establish what the common ground and shared challenge is. Create a core partnership or network for change.

2. **Scan and experience** the wider landscape for emerging signals and trends of change. Understand how the systems work and clarify the essential questions. Do not just analyse the situation: sense it, observe, listen and question by going out and experiencing it. Be ready to spot windows of opportunity for change.

3. Find approaches that help actors who seek change **connect to a living systems** perspective. This can often mean helping them articulate their purposes and align them to this perspective. That way, they can let go of the patterns that keep us unsustainable and envision future intentions and goals.

4. **Create experiments** and projects that mobilise people and develop prototypes of the new. Build and incubate these niches through networks that learn, finding a rhythm that creates new practices together.

5. Create **innovation and learning support structures**, such as communities of practice that build bridges from the niche to the mainstream. Connect innovations, actors and organisations together so that practices start to self-organise and diffuse. Support the actors in playing an active role in engaging their peers and translating their ideas to others.

6. Consolidate the change through **communicating** a coherent story that helps make the case that change is inevitable. Find mechanisms to bring together disparate activity so that it starts

to multiply and create additive change. Continually monitor what is happening at all levels so you are ready to capitalise on the windows of opportunity. Actively open up these windows by influencing the wider cultural conversation.

I will refer back to these strategies throughout the book and examples of how organisations are implementing them can be found in the next chapter.

The theories

A multi-level view of sustainability transitions[11]

As seen above a living systems perspective means we need to see systems as nested wholes embedded within each other. This nested perspective can be simplified into a multi-level view.

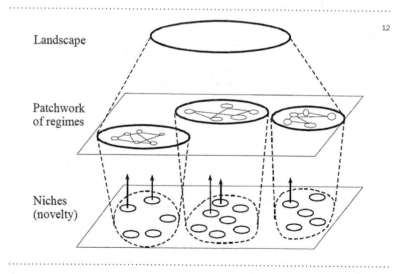

- The landscape level represents the changes in the wider environment and the socio-cultural shifts over time.

- The patchwork of regimes is at the mid-level (or sub-systems and sectors) of the wider landscape. These regimes share routines and rules and describe the current mainstream, such as the way we meet our current food and energy needs.

- The niche areas are where radical novelties are just emerging, often unstable and found at the fringe of the mainstream.

Analysing past system shifts or transitions across society has given us an understanding of how these three levels might interact to create change or a sustainability transition.[13]

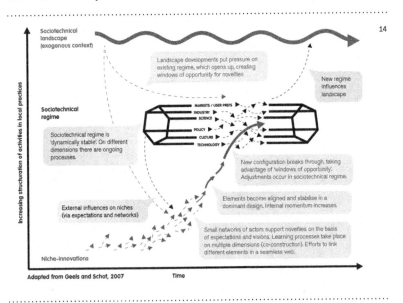

Adapted from Geels and Schot, 2007

System change or a transition can occur in many different ways. New niches, such as organic food, demonstrate viable alternatives to the current mainstream. This can lead mainstream retailers to adjust their behaviour and adopt these niche practices. These innovations, technologies or businesses can either offer a new way to fulfil our needs or replace one that already exists.

Wider landscape changes can put pressure on the mainstream to make changes. As political revolutions swept across Europe in the mid-nineteenth century, there was increasing emigration and demand for safer ships; with technological innovations this led to the shift from sailing to steam. Just as electrification led to innovations such as electric trams, so the current landscape developments in digital are allowing new models of businesses to grab this opportunity and become the new mainstream players. This is leading to some businesses failing whilst others rise (see for example the demise of HMV and the rise of Amazon).

Digital demonstrates how the niche or fringe is finding ways to influence the wider landscape shifts. This can happen as part of a wider cultural conversation, for example, through arts that capture the zeitgeist or campaigns or movements that create a media storm such as the Arab Spring.

As multiple parts change the mainstream reconfigures. This is what happened in the food system with the move from traditional farms to mass production in factories.

In terms of sustainability being the new norm or mainstream, this reconfiguration, or system change, has not yet occurred. If we look again at organic food, although it has been adopted by the mainstream as an option for consumers, it is still a niche in the agricultural and food sector, delivering only 1.5% of sales of food produce in the UK[15] and much less globally.

It is neither individuals, social forces nor the environment and infra-structure that shape society but the interaction between them. People make society and are at the same time constrained by it. Change is the ongoing process of mutual interaction, creating patterns and structures over time.[16]

Strategies for taking a multi-level view

Taking a nested or multi-level view helps you understand the structure and dynamics of systems change. It requires us to look for strategies that:

- Scan the landscape and regime for weak signals and windows of opportunities to effect change (**2**)

- Build the niches so they influence the regime and build bridges between the two. This might include supporting multiple innovations and the coming together of ideas to multiply the change (**5**); and

- Actively open up windows of opportunity through influencing the wider cultural conversation (**6**).

(These boxes recap and link back to the strategies on pages 27–29. The number indicates which one it relates to.)

A shift over time – the s-curve

To take a living systems perspective is to understand that system change does not happen linearly but more through a shift, or a tipping of the system. As relationships reconfigure the system moves from one state, or mainstream, to another. This shift can be represented by an s-curve.

Indicator of system change

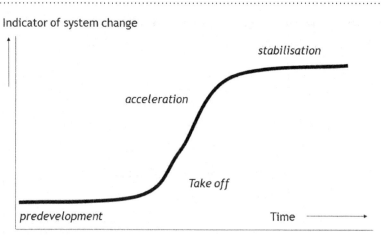

SOURCE: Kemp et al. (2007).

This s-curve has been used to understand the diffusion of innovation.[17] An innovation or new practice starts with a phase of very little change, where the adoption, take up or influence of the new practice is still held in the niches. As new relationships are formed there is a rapid take off where the system shifts. The curve represents the cumulative nature of adoption and market penetration. At the tipping point a critical mass has been reached and the change can become self-sustaining. This is of course unless other feedback processes and innovations divert this process.

We often do not know what exactly will cause this shift to occur and the current system often has vested interests maintaining the status quo. At the beginning of cultivating change it often feels like you are not getting anywhere. A search and learn process is therefore required to find ways to overcome these inhibiting factors.

Strategies for transition management

Transition management requires a search and learn process.

- Work through the problem with a group of front-runners to create a core group (**1**)

- Develop visions and strategies for taking it forward as a network (**2**)

- Execute experiments and projects that mobilise people and organisations (**4**)

- Monitor and evaluate the transition process to support take-off (**5**)

- Ensure partnerships, coalitions and networks are formed to start to create a social movement (**6**)

Supporting actors change systems – an effective leverage point

'Never doubt that a small group of thoughtful, committed citizens can change the world; indeed, it's the only thing that ever has'
MARGARET MEAD

One way to understand where to place your energy is by assessing what might have the greatest impact on the system. Leverage points are points where a small amount of energy might have a larger effect. If we start by trying to rebuild massive structures such as our transport system it might feel like an impossible task. However, if we can change the information flows in a system about how we use transport or the rules such as the transport policy we might have more effect. Meadows suggests that the most effective way to change the system is to shift the perspectives of a group of committed pioneers.[18]

Although system change happens through the reconfiguring of relationships and dynamics between multiple levels, this shift does not happen with everyone all at the same time. Different people choose to be a part of the change or resist it.

The s-curve can also represent the uptake and adoption of the new practices over time. If we break the population up into different groups according to the likelihood of their being a part of the change it can look like this:

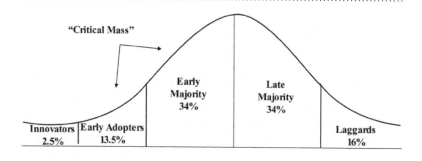

Critical to system change is not so much who comes up with the new ideas or innovations but the early adopters or pioneers who are able to take, translate and adapt these ideas for the mainstream, so that that a critical mass of change and relationships can be created.

We are all watching each other; if we look at our social groups we are likely to be surrounded by people who hold the same or similar perspectives as ourselves. A lot of our social cues come from those we associate with. We need to therefore find people who can translate, influence and communicate to the wider majority. Convincing early adopters or leaders in a field to take up new ideas and innovation becomes crucial in reaching the mainstream. These early adopters, pioneers and cultivators of change are the actors we need to engage.

In *The Tipping Point*, Malcolm Gladwell[19] writes about this viral influence. He identifies three types of people who are can support and build the critical mass:

- Connectors, or people who are really well networked

- Mavens, or the people you trust to analyse the best options for you

- Salespeople who help translate and tell a great story so as to get the message across.

This translation process is critical in moving from a few to many. Ideas and innovations have to be more compelling or have an advantage over what else is on offer. They must be simple so that people can understand them and be compatible with the adopter's or mainstream's current perspectives. We have to find ways to transfer the ideas between different contexts and allow trialling and adaption as we go along.

Strategies for supporting the people who are building the system

- Support the frontrunners and help them become actors who play an active role in engaging their peers and translating the ideas and practices for them (**1**)

- Identify the different actors in a system, especially those who have multiplying power: for example, professional bodies or specialist networks (**1**)

- Find strategies to build bridges between the fringe and the mainstream – especially through cultivating communities of practice that grow the processes of translation (**5**)

- Support the communication of a coherent story, bringing together disparate parts to demonstrate that change is already happening and that the shift is inevitable (**6**)

Cultivating relationships through communities of practice

We have created social support systems and infrastructures that lock us into unsustainable behaviours. Transformational ideas alone will not create the change. Social support structures are required to enable experiments and to ensure we learn from them. To make our behaviours sustainable, the social support systems and infrastructures need to change.

As system change practitioners we need to be more aware of the relationships between things. This can often require the cultivating of relationships and groups to support the shift. In system change, social learning can be used as a way to create transformational leaders and practice as well as sustaining and knitting together both emerging and mature practices.

We can learn from the facilitation of multi-stakeholder processes[20] and communities of practice as ways to create long-lasting change.

Communities of practice are groups of people who share a concern, a set of problems, or a passion about a topic, and who deepen their knowledge and expertise in these areas by interacting on an ongoing basis.[21]

The coordinators (or 'stewards') play a critical role in cultivating a community of practice. We rarely value the art and skill of linking the community together and fostering its development. Without a healthy community there is little lasting change. The role of cultivating the community of practice also involves actively managing the boundary between the community and the wider organisations and systems it is a part of.

Seven principles for cultivating communities of practice

- Design for evolution

- Open a dialogue between inside and outside perspectives

- Invite different levels of participation

- Develop private and public spaces

- Focus on what people value

- Combine familiarity and excitement

- Create a rhythm for the community

SOURCE: Wenger (2002)

Ensuring the appropriate learning process and support is an important element of success in system change, creating communities of practice that also inquire through taking action. The field of action inquiry and systemic action research can help us explore this in more detail.[22]

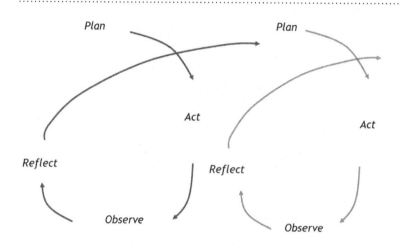

Strategies to cultivate communities of practice

- Prepare and find the potential people and common ground (**1**)

- Coalesce and pilot new practices together (**4**)

- Find a rhythm for the community to learn such as events and online communication. *Caution do not spend too much time on documenting information, it is more important to practise together* (**5**)

- As the community matures, expand, diffuse and connect

with others. Create a (self-organising) learning infrastructure based on what has and has not worked and invite others to join (**5**)

- The community needs to be stewarded and consolidated so that it has formal legitimacy and status in order that new members are recruited (in some cases this might be the forming of a new business or organisation) (**6**)

Creating transformational practices and leaders

There are different levels of learning that can help us understand how we might transform our perspective.

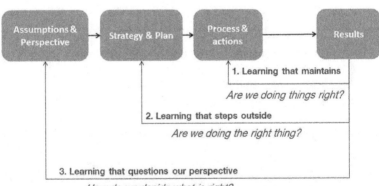

SOURCE: Based on Fisher et al. (2003).

It is the third level of questioning that supports a shift in consciousness or attention towards transformation.

Asking the questions about what the current purpose of the system is and what it might be if it was aligned with the living system as a whole can support system change. There are a variety of other approaches that support leaders to operate at this third level: one such model is Theory U.

In *Theory U* Scharmer[23] explains how a group of people in the German Health system were having a dialogue about the current system. Through interviews and conversation they observed that the current health system's behaviour and purpose was aligned to managing illness. When they started to connect to what would enable life they started to articulate how they might shift to a system that supports the health of society.

Freeing ourselves to ask this question and shift our perspective is harder than this example might suggest. Theory U is one model that system change practitioners use to help people act from the 'underlying process behind deep change and of enabling the enacting of such change processes'.[24] It offers a clear, coherent and well-organised process that helps us shift our perspective.

At the heart of this transformation is finding ways to access a deeper understanding of the living system. As individuals we are part of the living system. We can therefore experience a living system perspective by experiencing it in ourselves.

> *Exercise: This concept can be very hard to understand by mind alone. One way to experience it is through noticing your own body at work. Take a moment away from reading this book, notice your breath, experience the flow of energy in your own body, your heartbeat, your growing and moving.*

This sensing the present – or presencing – has been described as encountering life at work within us.[25] It requires us to find practices that help people see the living system and articulate their underlying purpose whilst letting go of current assumptions and behaviours.

1. Co-initiating:
uncover common intent
stop and listen to others and to
what life calls you to do

5. Co-evolving:
embody the new in ecosystems
that facilitate acting
from the whole

2. Co-sensing:
observe, observe, observe
connect with people and places
to sense the system from the whole

4. Co-creating:
prototype the new
in living examples to explore
the future by doing

3. Presencing:
connect to the source of inspiration and will
go to the place of silence and allow the inner knowing to emerge

SOURCE: Presencing Institute – Otto Scharmer

Strategies for cultivating transformational leaders and practice

- Bring together a diverse core group who share a common intention or problem (**1**)

- Clarify essential questions and go on learning journeys by visiting different on-the-ground examples to observe, listen and experience what is happening (**2**)

- Find practices that help people connect to a living systems perspective and articulate their purpose so as to help them let go of the patterns that keep us in the current system (**3**)

- Crystallise your vision and intention as a core group and prototype examples of a new way of doing things (**4**)

- Create infrastructures that support and continually connect to a living systems perspective (**5**)

Question: Which models and strategies above attract you and why? Which ones might you use?

This chapter has highlighted a number of strategies that illuminate what it might mean to make real a living systems perspective.

Remain open

As we become more deliberate in cultivating system change these strategies are only to support actions and are not blueprints. The map is not the territory; it is just that some strategies are more useful than others. If we take a living systems perspective then we need to take on an open, ever-changing sense of how change occurs, recognising that it is not linear or rational. Learning underpins all these and is vital whatever strategy you take.

Question: What are the assumptions you are making behind your strategies for change? What are their limitations?

In order to really understand how to cultivate system change we need to practise it. The next chapter will start to show some organisations' first steps into practising the art of cultivating system change. I then give my own reflections from my practice in the form of tips and insights into how we might navigate our way.

....

CHAPTER 3

Examples of Action

Can you take a deliberate approach to change?

CHANGE HAPPENS WITH OR WITHOUT YOU; even if you choose to do nothing, things will happen. There is debate, therefore, about whether system change is something you can deliberately create. We know a single organisation cannot create a system outcome and it does not happen overnight. This does not mean, however, that organisations cannot play a role in initiating the change.

This chapter will explore some organisations' initiatives for system change to stimulate your thoughts on how you might activate different strategies for change. It includes organisations that are non-profit and profit seeking, foundations and new emerging forms of organisation, for example, Labs.[26] It is only a small sample of the growing number of people who are starting to roll up their sleeves and get their hands dirty.

Question: What questions do you have about change? What would you like to learn from other organisations?

1. Bring together actors around a common challenge

As noted, system change is not something that happens through one person's or organisation's actions. It is in the coming together of people and organisations that the magic happens. Building partnerships for change is no small matter. At Forum for the Future we build from our network of partners, who are already leading the way in sustainability and starting to build coalitions and collaborations for change.

For instance, it took over three years for Forum to set up the Sustainability Shipping Initiative (**www.forumforthefuture.org/project/sustainable-shipping-initiative/overview**) as an independent organisation. It started from conversations aligning between different organisations and the setting up of a core group of five companies. These organisations saw the need to do something to improve their industry and realised it could not be done alone. This first wave acted as an attractor to other participants to build a collaborative venture seeking system change across the shipping industry with over 20 organisations. Relationship and trust building was critical, as was senior level engagement. This in-depth process will hopefully sustain the group through the murky waters of change still to come. Experienced facilitation is invaluable to forming and developing a group.

System innovation: Forum for the Future

Forum for the Future is a sustainability non-profit organisation, working globally with business, government and others to solve tricky challenges through system innovation. We have created our framework – '6 steps to significant change' – as a useful starting point for us and others to develop new ways of creating change.

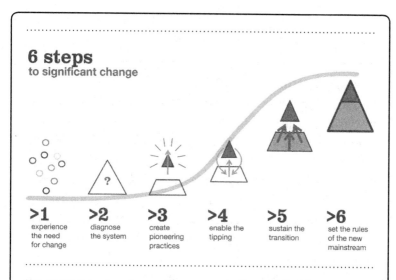

6 steps
to significant change

>1 experience the need for change

>2 diagnose the system

>3 create pioneering practices

>4 enable the tipping

>5 sustain the transition

>6 set the rules of the new mainstream

We suggest system innovation occurs in the middle of this change cycle and includes diagnosing the system through to the point at which the change has momentum and is starting to tip. These steps are often the hardest to understand and are therefore overlooked by change agents as it is difficult to see where to start and how to grow the impact to a wider range of actors. This is also where the magic can happen and is critical for achieving a long-lasting impact.

As the business case begins to be made and the imperative made more real by environmental and social pressures, we are starting to see businesses exploring what system change means for their sustainability strategies. Nike is one of the first businesses to be explicit about creating system change and there are many others who have been doing work in this area, such as Unilever working with the Marine Stewardship Council or Kingfisher working with the Forest Stewardship Council where both bodies are looking for wider industry change.

Market transformation: Nike

In 2009 Nike announced a new model of working as part of their plan to shift to a sustainable business. This included fast-tracking the integration of sustainability into its business, as well as developing scalable solutions to enable a closed-loop business model. Many other businesses are trying to embed sustainability as part of their core business but Nike are among the first to realise the need to innovate and move beyond their organisational boundary and start to shape the systems they are a part of. To do this they have three strategies: to innovate, integrate into the business and mobilise wider system innovation.

Nike recognised they were part of a complex value chain and, following Greenpeace's Detox Campaign demanding toxic-free fashion, they helped initiate the Road to Zero project (www.roadmaptozero.com). Nike led the industry to embrace zero discharge of hazardous chemicals by 2020 – alongside Adidas, Puma, C&A, H&M and China's Li Ning. This coalition did some work mapping how toxic chemicals occur in their supply chain, how the value chain interrelates, who the stakeholders are, and the inherent power dynamics. This was used to create and stress test their strategy and deepen collaborative efforts.

However, just working with the 'big' players or current mainstream players is not the only route to system change. We need to find the leaders of the future who might disrupt and create new forms and systems. In the Finance Innovation Lab they are trying to find ways to connect with these leaders in supportive communities to accelerate the emergence of new values and to aggregate influence. They have created Fellows who are leaders and practitioners of system change to form collaborative projects and have brought together different communities, like audit professionals (**http:// thefinancelab.org/auditfutures/**) to engage in dialogues about the future.

System change requires us to work at evolving the current system and disrupting it with the new. Different partnerships and collaborations need to be formed: some might be large, some small, some might be with the mainstream, some with the new players, some open and collaborative and others may be highly competitive. We need a mixture of them all.

2. Scan and experience what is happening to find opportunities for change

One of the effective ways to identify common challenges, establish the current state of the system and also lay the ground for innovation is through the use of futures techniques. In Dairy 2020 (**www.forumforthefuture. org/project/dairy-2020/overview**) Forum for the Future bought together organisations right across the supply chain. Together they co-created possible future scenarios for the dairy industry. Using these, the group agreed a vision for a sustainable dairy industry and developed a framework of guiding principles for how we can get there.

Futures and a large network of people can also be used to **scan the world** and crowd-source where problems are coalescing and demonstrating a window of opportunity for change. This approach is a core part of how The Rockefeller Foundation makes decisions about where to invest. Taking this future-oriented perspective ensures they can understand the landscape and be ready to find challenges and ideas across the systems and explore questions they are interested in.

Philanthropic innovation: The Rockefeller Foundation

The Rockefeller Foundation promotes the well-being of humanity and addresses the needs of the poor through expanding opportunity and building resilience. They use innovation, influence and intervention to achieve impact across issues such as revaluing ecosystems, advancing health, securing livelihoods and transforming cities.

It takes a systems based approach to philanthropy. The Foundation seeks to understand the context of the problem within a system, frame the goal and devise a strategy that leverages comparative advantage in deploying resources to drive sustainable change. It works across sectors, governments, private and civil society in order to scale up social innovation into large-scale change.

One area Rockefeller focused on was the challenge of growing cities in the developing world. The informal city, that is the part of the city not in the formal economy, is where most of this growth is and yet is excluded from regulation and support. The Informal City Dialogue project (**http://nextcity.org/informalcity**) is a global, multi-stakeholder project fostering a conversation about the role of informality in creating inclusion and resilience in future cities. It uses futures work and innovation to work across six cities: Accra, Bangkok, Chennai, Lima, Manila and Nairobi. The project involves a diverse group of citizens developing future scenarios of what life in their city could be like in 2040. It seeks to foster positive change in communities and institutions, as well as policies and practice, through encouraging innovations that will help cities build on the strengths of the informal city to achieve a resilient future. These stories (**www.rockefellerfoundation.org/blog/three-short-films-informal-cities**) will be taken to a broader audience, engaging the whole city in a conversation as well as reaching out to the wider world. Futures can therefore be very helpful when looking at strategy 6: communicating the stories of change.

As well as futures techniques being used to engage actors in understanding the challenge and make informed decisions, there are other systemic inquiry methods that include sustainability frameworks, systems maps (**www. forumforthefuture.org/project/framework-sustainable-economy/overview**) and supporting people to experience the current, and scenarios of a possible future, world.

The Sustainable Food Lab

The mission of the Sustainable Food Lab is to accelerate the shift to sustainable food, from niche to mainstream. It is a consortium of business, non-profit and public organisations, for example, Mars, Oxfam and The World Bank, working together to accelerate the shift toward sustainability. It was initiated in 2004 by convening a leadership group of about 30 where each organisation signed up for two years to understand sustainability from each other's perspective and jointly investigate what they could do together and then kick-start pilot projects and collaborative partnerships. From this is it now an organisation continuing to create change across the food system.

In the Sustainable Food Lab they take their consortium of organisations on regular learning journeys to offer opportunities for cross-sector dialogue. In May 2012 the Lab took a group to Santo Domingo to visit cocoa farms, cooperatives, producers, manufacturers and an exporter as well an eco-tourism enterprise and agro-forestry reserve. Getting a picture of the current reality is very important in finding innovative solutions for the future.

A large part of the Sustainable Food Lab's work is creating a safe and productive space in which dialogue can lead to innovation. These journeys provide the backbone to their innovation pilots and leadership development as well as creating insights and analysis of what is happening in the field that they can communicate more widely.

3. Align our visions and purposes to a living system perspective

As well as learning journeys, the Sustainable Food Lab takes its members into the wilderness to explore group and solo experiences in order to access the deeper wisdom of feeling a fuller connection to ourselves and the planet. This process can challenge participants to abandon old assumptions and initiatives and find the will to lead systems change.

Connecting to purpose and to life also underpins the Finance Lab's work. They find it can awaken a sense of curiosity and urgency to act. This is not exemplified by a single project but through the way that they operate as a core stewardship team across their projects and is seen as vital to creating the necessary shift across the finance system.

> ### The Finance Innovation Lab[27]
> The Finance Innovation Lab is jointly hosted by WWF-UK and ICAEW (the Institute of Chartered Accountants in England and Wales). It was launched in 2008 as an incubator for systems change in finance.

The Finance Lab does this in three ways:

- They incubate new business models, innovation within the mainstream and new forms of civil society.

- They accelerate the capacity of leaders to create change.

- They create the wider conditions for change by raising awareness, creating supportive communities and advocating for policy change.

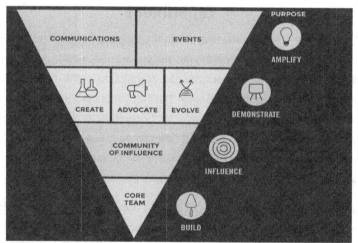

Our strategy for systems change. Level 1, we amplify good ideas and connect the community, Level 2 we demonstrate what alternatives look like, Level 3 we influence and Level 4 the Core Team build the strategy

They work with people from a broad spectrum of backgrounds, including mainstream finance, the creative industries, academia, NGOs and those seeking alternative business and finance models.

Many initiatives invent visions and roadmaps to support them in creating change. What a living system perspective requires us to do is question the aspiration and goals for the system change. Does the vision maintain the current system, where a goal of more growth is based on an ever-increasing ecological resource, or does it orientate towards a sustainable future? The Food and Finance Labs demonstrate how this has been done through a personal connection to ecology and each other. We need to explore how this alignment can be reached for different people in different ways.

4. Experiment

Labs are great places to experiment. In the Finance Innovation Lab they created UnLtd Future a programme designed to accelerate alternative business models and connect people, planet and profit. It supported nine entrepreneurs with sustainable business models through monthly meetings to build capacity followed up by mentoring and peer-to-peer support. Generating and incubating new niches is seen as an important way to create completely new innovations for change – as the system change is not going to be based on repeating what we have today.

However, experimentation does not have to occur just in Labs. There are many other organisations trying to experiment with ways to create impact towards major sustainability and development issues.

Market solutions at scale: Shell Foundation

Shell Foundation has ambitious objectives to catalyse scalable and sustainable solutions to global developmental challenges and have set about doing this by taking a pioneering enterprise-based approach – meaning they seek to achieve long-term financial viability rather than subsidy solutions.

Key to their approach is to see ways to create long-term partnerships and build market-based solutions that seek leverage for scale and sustainability into the future.

At Shell Foundation they have sought to do this through building pioneers through strategic partnerships such as EMBARQ which acts as an independent broker and aims to improve the quality of life of people living in mega-cities. It does this through implementing sustainable transport solutions to improve the quality of life in these cities or through The Better Trading Company which acts as an ethical intermediary to help build sustainable supply chains that help eradicate poverty.

Through analysing the market and building networks and partnerships they were able to pilot a number of different projects that would help address the challenges they had identified, for example, access to energy or sustainability mobility. By incubating ideas they were able to select one pioneer to partner with – and invest in – and then support activities to help them scale up success, support replication of the model and find ways to catalyse the adoption of their approach. All this whilst continually being transparent and learning what works and which other areas require a different strategy or effort.

Experiments are happening in many places, from entrepreneurs creating new products and services, to government agencies finding new ways to do development or support innovation, and foundations looking at new forms and organisational models. Although there is a lot going on, what is vital for any organisation's strategy is to ensure they are both transformational *and* that we learn from and evolve our approaches for greater impact.

5. Create innovation and learning support structures to translate, bridge and diffuse change

Shell Foundation have experimented and set up a number of enterprises. However, when your ambitions are system-wide there are limits to what one innovation or enterprise can achieve. This is why the Foundation has been looking at how they address market enablers through catalysing businesses such as Dharma who have created a rural distribution network in India to serve the 'bottom of the pyramid' – providing products and services that are socially affordable. It also provides income-generation opportunities for rural entrepreneurs. They have co-founded with the UN Foundation the Global Alliance for Cook Stoves to create a thriving global market for clean and efficient household cooking solutions by enhancing demand, strengthening supply and providing an enabling environment in the market through research and engagement.

These types of organisation are starting to find ways to bridge the gap by building an infrastructure for wider impact.

NIKE recognises the need to mobilise key constituents (civil society, employees, consumers, government and industry) to partner in scaling up solutions. They are partnering with NASA, USAID and the US State Department to accelerate a revolution in sustainable materials through LAUNCH2020. This is founded on a simple idea: you need to scale innovation for impact by utilising networks, strategies and resources and bringing them together for change.

To see the LAUNCH process in full go to **http://www.launch.org/process**

The centrepiece is a Summit of multi-disciplinary leaders and stake-holders whose expertise, networks and resources will chart the course of action for these innovations. In May 2013, 150 high-profile people were brought together to play a game to help people think systemically and make investments for sustainability over time. It started the process of collaboration and inspired innovative ideas.

The next step is for ideas and initiatives that came out of the LAUNCH Summit to be submitted to the incubation process, where 10 will be scaled. The accelerator programme hopes to strengthen the strategies, expand the networks and resource and amplify the impact of the innovations.

As we have seen, there are many ways these initiatives are trying to bridge the future and the present. For example, the Sustainable Shipping Initiative (**www.forumforthefuture.org/project/sustainable-shipping-initiative/ more/ssi-work-streams**) has now been set up as an independent entity so it can provide a support structure around the innovation work-streams to move towards implementation and scale.

As we aim to create greater impact across systems,we need to better understand how to scale up our impact. We need to explore better what forms of cross-system learning, innovation, collaborations and digital platforms might help to accelerate change across different systems.

6. Communicate a coherent story and open up windows to influence wider change

To support this acceleration we need to open up opportunities for influence. Traditionally organisations like Greenpeace have raised awareness of the problems and push organisations to act as seen above with their Detox campaign. However, we need to find sophisticated communication approaches that not only point to the negative effects of our behaviour but also start to consolidate and influence the wider cultural conversation.

In Forum for the Future's Community Energy Coalition (**www.forumfor thefuture.org/project/community-energy-coalition/overview**) we created a coalition with influencers in society, such as the Woman's Institute and the Church of England. This was to both to reach a wider base of people and to influence policy. The project is now looking to develop an energy conversation to change the story about the energy consumer's role in the energy market.

Other exciting examples of initiatives looking to do this include The Story of Stuff (**http://storyofstuff.org**) first creating movies that question why we want more and how we throw away stuff in our lives, then creating a movement of change-makers and campaigns to communicate a clear message. The Virgin Unite Foundation have employed a storyteller to help communicate the work of their entrepreneurs; the SMART CSOs (**www.smart-csos.org**) initiative is trying to understand the cultural transformation required for The Great Transition from our current paradigm to the next; and The Comms Lab are looking at how the television and advertising system can help address the environmental and social challenges we face.

A growing number of examples

Thus there are more and more organisations and initiatives trying to activate strategies for systems change – from those that have been established for a while in the Academy for systemic change (**www.academyforchange. org**) and Reos alongside those seeding new areas for system change such as Nesta's (**www.nesta.org.uk/publications/assets/features/systems_ innovation_discussion_paper**) work on ageing (**www.nesta.org.uk/press_ releases/assets/features/five_hours_a_day**), the Volans Breakthrough program (**www.volans.com/project/breakthrough-capitalism/**), Golden's Ecosystems Labs (**goldenforsustainability.org**) and the TNS Canada Sustainability Transition Labs (**www.naturalstep.ca/sustainability-transition-lab**). This is to only name a few as the field keeps expanding.

The examples here demonstrate the different priorities and emphasis people and organisations have in terms of their strategies and initiatives. Some focus more on working with the current 'power and influence' in the system, or indeed *are* the current power trying to evolve from within, while others are creating and incubating new innovations that question the premise and goal of the current market and system. Some of the examples might feel like they are just improving the current system instead of changing it. What is important is how these different strategies come together as a whole to create a shift in the system.

If we take a living system perspective we need to make clear which goal we are working towards. Many initiative's goals might be making improvements but are still perpetuating the goal of driving consumption rather than aligning the solutions to support the living planet as a whole.[28] The exploration of strategy 3, aligning our visions and goals to a living system perspective, needs to both be further explored and made more explicit.

If we are to assume we need a mix of actions across all six strategies then we need more of strategies 5 and 6. Creating platforms and communicating a new narrative for our society for a wider movement are not easy strategies to implement as they require us to stay in the game for much longer. They are therefore harder to fund but are going to be vitally important in accelerating our collective effort.

A living system perspective means we need to constantly learn and evolve our actions and, in seeking to explore the relationships between our initiatives, to see how these different approaches are adding up towards system change at the economic and societal levels.

Question: What strategies are you focusing on? What action can you take?

The fun starts when you get stuck in. The next chapter will give you some things to watch for on your way as you convene, experience, connect, experiment, learn and communicate.

....

CHAPTER 4

Navigating Your Way

I THINK OF GETTING MY YOUNG CHILDREN ready in the morning, having to find strategies, rules, rewards, so that they get dressed. You compromise on blue or red socks, sometimes you even let them wear their Spiderman outfits, but ultimately the goal is the same – to leave the house with a dressed child. Navigating system change feels the same at times, working with the grain, pushing points that matter. Ultimately we are trying to

reach the same desired goal of a sustainable future but we also realise we are only one person in a world of many.

There is no perfect example of how to create change. In the last chapter we saw how organisations are attempting it. This chapter changes focus on to you and me as individual agents for change. The practice of system change is messy but we need to get started.

Learning our way through

There is no Holy Grail or silver bullet to determine what will shift a system. At the heart of living systems lies novelty and the feedback processes that enable us to adapt. Without this learning there is no life. Learning and experimentation is not just about emergence – the premise of this book is that it also can be cultivated.

Get started

People think learning has to be strenuous. Let me let you into a secret, it doesn't. Experimenting and learning follows who you are and what you love doing. It does not have to involve much more than what you are already doing. Here are a few things to turn learning from unnoticed to productive.

1. **Name your questions and strategies**

   Question: What are your questions? What are your strategies for change?

2. **Do something – experiment.**

   No matter how small. For example, try a new way of saying something. Pay attention to what you are doing.

   Question: How can you pay attention to your actions, strategies, assumptions or perspectives? What will you do tomorrow?

3. **Collect insights from your experience**

   - How do you record notes from meetings – do you have a favourite book? (This is a picture of mine.)

- What do you tweet about? Do you record them elsewhere?

- What insights do you get from just talking with people in meetings or over lunch?

Question: What do you love doing and are doing already? How are you collecting insights and ideas?

4. Find the patterns – reflect

This is the bit we often do not do; finding the patterns in your insights. Can you schedule 30 minutes a week or even per month to look back at what you have learnt? Some people do this through blogs or even more creative ways like mind-mapping.

Question: What have you noticed recently that could be your first insight into cultivating change? What challenges do you keep coming up against?

5. Re-question and plan

Having found a new insight what are you going to do differently? What new questions do you have?

The flow overleaf is the basis of action inquiry. There are other more detailed approaches in action research such as systemic action research where we might seek to follow inquiry streams in multiple places and respond to the complex challenges that lie at the heart of these projects.[29]

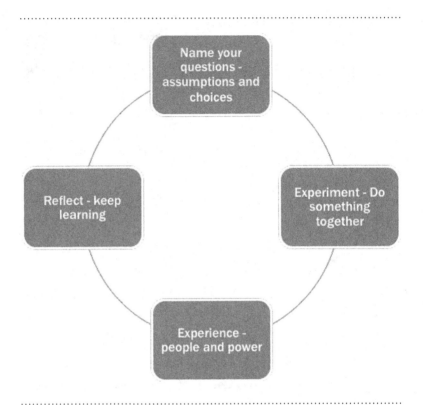

In the System Innovation Lab we are seeking to find ways to experiment and learn through system change projects. The first step however is feeling what it is like to learn as an individual and to navigate your own way.

This chapter therefore explores some of the lessons I have encountered when working with different people, organisations and systems. They might not be the same for you, but I hope by presenting them here you might recognise something in your own practice and we can start to help each other improve our skills of navigating systems change.

Question

Name your assumptions

Innovation is often seen as the answer to many a problem, but what if our innovation processes are part of the problem not the solution? Currently a lot of innovation is driving the growth in material consumer goods, requiring the use of more and more resources. Our growing obesity problem stems in part from innovations in the food sector or from urban planning. However, we seek to

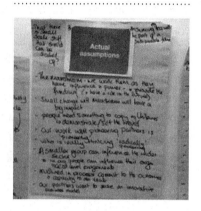

This image is a list of assumptions recorded from a team away-day.

innovate solutions in the health system rather than asking what the root causes of consumption are.

When we make choices about which strategy we wish to use it is important to recognise why we have made them. Sometimes we only see and hear the things that confirm what we already know. Without knowing where one is coming from how can you remain open to others?

Naming our assumptions and therefore what perspective we are working from can help us break free and innovate for system change rather than business as usual.

Question: What assumptions have you made? What wider goals and perspectives are your projects and innovations serving?

Know yourself – holding the whole world in your hands

Crucial to naming your assumptions is the need to know yourself as a change agent.

I was sitting with a friend, my four-month-old baby was at home with his father and I was struggling; I really couldn't cope with the shift and transition to parenthood. She turned to me and asked: 'what is the approach you take when working with people in your job?' I looked at her strangely as if to say 'what has that got to do with being a mother?' But as I replied and heard myself saying that I provide the space for others to learn and grow it started to all fall into place, that I did not have to do everything for this little child just provide a good enough space.

Finding out who we are and what we want to work on can be a process that lasts a lifetime. It is a line between the very personal and the very public – sustainability requires us to explore this full spectrum.

As a practitioner of system change I have spent time both trying to understand not just the strategies we need but also the kind of person I want to be and how that relates to me as a living being on this planet – how does my job, my life, my work contribute?

Understanding your role, your influence and also how that relates to the bigger picture can be very empowering. Exploring purposes can work at a personal level but can be used as a tool for teams, organisations and systems.

Question: Where do you stand? Who are you and what is your life's work?

One simple way to start to unpack this question is through drawing a circle that names what you are concerned about, the things that feel too big for you to address or work on and then to draw a smaller circle in the middle[30] that represents your sphere of influence and what you have around you – then think what can I do that helps expand my sphere of influence?

Make choices

Knowing where you are coming from and the assumptions you are making can help you make choices about where to place your energy. Navigating your way through different systems is all about making choices. Deciding if something is a success or not often depends on how you define and put the boundary of the system. Looking at the example of organic food in Chapter 2, if we wanted to change the food system we might not have succeeded but if we were looking at a smaller objective then possibly we have created change in retailers' behaviour and practice.

My choice as a change agent has been to support pioneers in taking a living system perspective and moving to action. My boundaries move, from myself, to my organisation through to sectors such as education and energy as well as supporting the system change community itself. Being clear about why you are making these choices helps you re-assess and improve.

Question: What choices are you making? Where are you best placed to put your energy?

Experiment – do something together

Demonstrate value

One of the challenges with playing between the lines of the current and new is finding the resources and space to create change. There is often a limited business case or viable funding model for creating value in the future based on what we have today.

Many organisations have a vested interest in the current system. However, without imagining how things can be different, many businesses and organisations fail as they were not able to re-invent themselves. Kodak, for example, did not adapt to the digital wave taking over photography and went bankrupt.

Creating something small that demonstrates your ambition can help you work towards your vision. One of my inquiries has been around the role of art as a space to communicate and engage people in a living systems perspective (strategy 6). With a friend and colleague I therefore created a small exhibition to experiment and demonstrate what this would look like.[31]

Question: What one thing can you do that demonstrates your ambition but is achievable in the short term?

Form supportive relationships and build new ones

You do not have to do it alone. Forming relationships around a shared endeavour can multiply your effect. You need to find people who you can call your team. However, for system change we also need to build new relationships and this can be a painful and tricky process. In one project we worked on a colleague of mine assessed that she had spent 60% cent of her time on cultivating relationships.

We have to recognise that we all have many roles and drivers. We often have responsibilities to our jobs and organisations and yet some people come into these processes because they are motivated on a personal level. In the Sustainable Shipping Initiative, there was a moment when the facilitator was finding it tough as the group were trying to agree on a vision. They were trying to see eye-to-eye on something that was both stretching but also offered targets their organisation could get behind. Navigating these politics has to be done with an awareness of not only who is in the room but also what is happening outside.

Experience

Dance with power

'You think I do crazy stuff you should meet the artists and radicals I hang out with – I am normal by their standards.'[32] Some days it feels like I am masquerading in many worlds; in the morning I will be walking into a big business and in the afternoon I will be in a conversation with people who are trying to bring them down. Wherever you go when working with systems change you are dancing with many flavours of power, making moves in different worlds and with different steps.

I come up against what I feel is an unnecessary divide between those who think system change has to come from the fringe and that the mainstream is all bad and those who are sitting in the mainstream and feel the hand grenades being lobbed across whilst trying to reach similar goals.

A person I know from the City walked down from their office block into the Occupy Movement and asked them how he could help with their cause, what could he take back to his colleagues? The person he was talking to just looked at him in amazement and told him he was missing the point. While putting these two worlds together is not necessarily the answer, it might stir things up and create opportunities – but it might also halt things in their tracks.

Working with the niche does not necessarily mean out of the mainstream, as seen with Nike and other partners Forum works with. It might be from people who are willing to create a new model of business or organisation. Many sustainability practitioners feel they are at the fringe of their own organisations and these strategies can equally apply to them. We are also seeing a growing number of senior leaders who are willing to question the system they are a part of. Unilever's CEO Paul Polman, for example,[33] is looking to find ways to question a finance system that is constraining their ability to implement their 'Sustainable Living Plan' (**www.unilever. co.uk/sustainable-living/**).

The examples above show how mainstream business is having a go, how new entrants are being incubated and made stronger, and how ways to bring these worlds together are being explored; there is an art to navigating a territory that lies in between, different dances for different people.

Question: What are the power dynamics in the systems you are working with? Who holds power and influence over a situation and what might create a counter move to this power?

Speak many languages

It was a sunny day. Fifty people were sitting in pairs on an embankment outside our conference. They were having a conversation about their concerns for the future, going deeper into their fears about the impact of climate change. On the feedback forms I received a comment that has stuck with me since. 'These exercises are like Marmite, you either love it or hate it.'

Cultivating system change is knowing how to push people that little bit further without losing them along the way. You have to ensure that you both work with different people's perspectives and preferences whilst also pushing them so they start to shift and change their perspective.

Remembering you are not alone often helps. If we take a living system perspective then building relationships and using these different perspectives can help. You might not be the right person or have the right approach to reach those you would like to work with whereas someone else could be.

The first step is to know who you are. A lot of the dance of change happens in working with the people you have in front of you. Find ways to know your audience, communicate to them and use others to translate and bring a growing number of people along. This skill is like learning to speak many languages.

Question: Who is your audience? Where are they coming from? Who do they listen to?

Reflect – keep learning

There is no such thing as failure – only feedback

Having a strategy does not mean you have created the change. When the Shell Foundation published a report looking at the lessons they have learnt over the past 10 years they highlighted the achievements they had made as well as being transparent about what had not worked and what more they needed to do. In the first two years, for example, they state that 80% of the initiatives they supported failed to achieve the scale or sustainability they were seeking. The Finance Innovation Lab in a blog (**www.nesta.org.uk/blogs/systemic_innovation_a_discussion_series/ the_finance_innovation_lab_a_case_study_of_system_innovation_in_ finance**) for NESTA showed the difference between their intentions and the reality on the ground when they got into the practice of system change.

Make it a habit

Learning is not something we do once, it is something we have to be constantly doing and sustaining. Moving an innovation from idea to prototype is a hard and long process. To scale up its impact takes even longer. Learning is not just the immediate summary of activity but an enduring process that has to have structure and a rhythm of activity.

....

Summary

THE CHALLENGES OF SUSTAINABILITY are becoming ever more urgent as we approach, even exceed, our ecological limits – a state of affairs which threatens our very survival. This awareness could paralyse us into inaction. The aim of this book, therefore, has been to help you find ways to move forward and explore how you might actively take a living systems perspective, see yourself as part of the world, unravel complex challenges, and find strategies for change by taking the necessary steps.

A living systems perspective requires us to view the whole system, see ourselves as part of the world, to work together and cultivate relationships and collaborations and be explicit in learning and making choices so we break the patterns of our current reality.

To do this we need to go out into the world and **experience** what is happening. We must find windows of opportunity and **people** and organisations willing to work with us on shared challenges. We need to **connect** to the living system and establish visions that can spark exciting **experiments**. We need to focus on the **learning** architecture that will help us transition and self-organise and find ways to hold a wider cultural **conversation** for more to come on board.

This journey is not one to be travelled alone. As more and more examples are created I look forward to hearing about the outcomes and insights you have along the way – please get in touch.

References

Bateson, G. 2002. *Mind and Nature: A Necessary Unity* (Cresskill, NJ: Hampton Press).

Burns, D. 2007. *Systemic Action Research: A Strategy for Whole System Change* (Bristol: Policy Press).

Capra, F. 1997. *The Web of Life: A New Synthesis of Mind and Matter* (London: HarperCollins).

Covey, S. 2004. *The 7 Habits of Highly Effective People: Powerful Lessons in Personal Change* (London: Simon & Schuster).

Fisher, D., Rooke, D. and Torbert, B. 2003. *Personal and Organizational Transformation through Action Inquiry* (Boston, MA: Edge/Work Press).

Geels, F.W. 2002. Technological transitions as evolutionary recon-figuration processes: A multi-level perspective and a case-study. *Research Policy* (Volume 31, Number 8/9): 1257–1274.

Geels, F.W. and Schot, J. 2010. The dynamics of transition: A socio-technical perspective. In J. Grin, J. Rotmans and J. Schot (eds) *Transitions to Sustainable Development: New Directions in the Study of Long Term Transformative Change* (New York: Routledge).

Giddens, A. 1984. *The Constitution of Society: Outline of the Theory of Structuration* (Cambridge: Polity Press).

Gladwell, M. 2000. *The Tipping Point: How Little Things Can Make a Big Difference* (New York: Abacus).

REFERENCES

Grin, J., Rotmans, J. and Schot, J., in collaboration with Geels, F. and Loorback, D. 2010. *Transitions to Sustainable Development: New Directions in the Study of Long Term Transformative Change* (New York: Routledge).

Harding, S. (2006) *Animate Earth: Science, Initiation and Gaia.* Green Books, Totnes

Hemmati, M. 2002. *Multi-stakeholder Processes for Governance and Sustainability: Beyond Deadlock and Conflict* (London: Earthscan).

Kemp, R., Loorbach, D. and Rotmans, J. 2007. Transition management as a model for mapping processes of co-evolution towards sustainable development. *International Journal of Sustainable Development and World Ecology* (Volume 14): 1–15.

Kolb, D.A. 1984. *Experiential Learning: Experience as the Source of Learning & Development* (Upper Saddle River, NJ: Prentice-Hall).

Macy, J. and Brown, M.Y. 1998. *Coming Back to Life: Practices to Reconnect Our Lives, Our World* (Gabriola Island, BC: New Society Publishers).

McIntosh, A. 2009. *Hell and High Water: Climate Change, Hope and the Human Condition* (Edinburgh: Birlinn).

Meadows, D. 1999. *Leverage Points: Places to Intervene in the System.* Sustainability Institute. **http://www.sustainer.org/pubs/Leverage_Points. pdf**

Meadows, D. 2009. *Thinking in Systems: A Primer* (London: Earthscan).

Reams, D. 2007. Illuminating the blind spot: An overview and response to Theory U. *Integral Review* (Volume 5): 249–259.

Reason, P. and Bradbury, H. 2006a. Introduction: Inquiry and participation in search of a world worthy of human aspiration. In P. Reason and H. Bradbury (eds) *Handbook of Action Research*, pp. 1–14 (London: SAGE).

Reason, P. and Bradbury, H. 2006b. Conclusion: Broadening the bandwidth of validity: Issues and choice-points for improving the quality of action research. In P. Reason and H. Bradbury (eds) *Handbook of Action Research*, pp. 343–351 (London: SAGE).

Reason, P., Coleman, G., Ballard, D., Williams, M., Gearty, M., Bond, C., Seeley, C. and Maughan McLachlan, D. 2009. *Insider Voices, Human Dimensions of Low Carbon Technology* (Bath: CARPP, University of Bath).

Rogers, E.M. 2005. *Diffusion of Innovation*, 5th edn (New York: Simon & Schuster).

Rotmans, J., Kemp, R. and van Asselt, M.B.A. 2001. More evolution than revolution. Transition management in public policy. *Foresight* (Volume 3, Number 1): 15–31.

Rudolph, J., Taylor, S. and Foldy, E. 2001. Collaborative off line reflection: A way to develop skill in action science and action inquiry. In P. Reason and H. Bradbury (eds) *Handbook of Action Research*, pp. 307–314 (London: SAGE).

Scharmer, C.O. 2007. *Theory U: Leading from the Future as it Emerges* (Cambridge: SOL).

Senge, P., Scharmer, C.O., Jaworski, J. and Flowers, B.S. 2005. *Presence: Exploring Profound Change in People, Organizations and Society* (London: Nicholas Brealey Publishing).

REFERENCES

Senge, P.M. 2006. *The Fifth Discipline: The Art of Practice and the Learning Organisation* (London: Random House).

Soil Association. 2013. Organic market report 2013, downloaded from **www.soilassociation.org**

Wenger, E. 1998. *Communities of Practice: Learning, Meaning and Identity* (Cambridge: Cambridge University Press).

Wenger, E., McDermott, R.A. and Snyder, W. 2002. *Cultivating Communities of Practice: A Guide to Managing Knowledge* (Cambridge, MA: Harvard Business School Press).
....

Notes

1. Meadows, 2009: 101.

2. Meadows, 2009: ix.

3. Notably the work of F. Capra in *The Web of Life*, 1997.

4. Drawn from Capra's work on living systems (1997) and Meadows's (2009) characteristics.

5. Meadows, 2009: 84.

6. Life being far from equilibrium also means we are moving towards ever increasing complexity (Capra, 1997: 176).

7. Capra, 1997: 222.

8. Harding, 2006: 76.

9. McIntosh, 2009: 7.

10. Harding, 2006.

11. Geels and Schot, 2010.

12. Geels, 2002.

13. A transition is a radical, structural change of a societal sub-system that is the result of a co-evolution of economic, cultural, technical, ecological and institutional developments at different scales and levels (Rotmans et al., 2001).

14. Reason et al., 2009.

15. Soil Association, 2013.

16. Giddens, 1984.

17. Rogers, 2005.

18. 1999.

19. Gladwell, 2000.

20. Hemmati, 2002.

21. Wenger et al., 2002: 4.

22. Fisher et al., 2003; Reason and Bradbury, 2006a, 2006b; Burns, 2007.

23. 2007: 136–142.

24. Reams, 2007.

25. Scharmer, 2007: 48.

26. Over the past five years there have been a number of Labs popping up trying to find ways to initiate change. This site pulls together an interesting collection of examples: http://www.societal-innovation.org/

27. Further details: http://thefinancelab.org/

28. The Story of Stuff video (http://youtu.be/cpkRvc-sOKk) explains this difference.

29. Burns, 2007.

30. Covey, 2004.

31. www.focus-out.tumblr.com

32. Quote picked up in conversation.

33. http://www.mckinsey.com/features/capitalism/paul_polman

Printed in the United States
by Baker & Taylor Publisher Services